COZY
MOUNTAIN
LODGE™

Worship Leader Guide

Real. **Bold.** Love.

Cozy Mountain Lodge Worship Leader Guide

Visit our websites: **group.com** and **group.com/women**

This resource is brought to you by the creative team at Group Publishing. Choose Group resources for women's ministry and experience the difference!

ISBN 978-1-4707-5354-2

Printed in the United States of America.

10 9 8 7 6 5 4 3 2 1   21 20 19 18

Contents

Welcome to Cozy Mountain Lodge!

Are you in need of a relaxing day in the mountains? Time to slow down, savor a warm beverage while chatting with friends, and enjoy the beauty of the great outdoors? Every woman longs for a day like this—even those who live hundreds of miles from the nearest mountain! That's why we created Cozy Mountain Lodge.

Cozy Mountain Lodge is a retreat where women slow down and enjoy time with other women and with God. It's an in-depth Bible study, an unforgettable worship experience, and an open invitation for women to draw closer together as they find shelter in God.

If you're reading this guide, it's likely you're leading worship during Cozy Mountain Lodge. The following pages will walk you through it all.

Your Contribution to Cozy Mountain Lodge

You play a key role in making women feel welcome and in guiding them in worship. Your key responsibilities at the retreat are:

❀ Greet women and lead them in worship for several of the sessions.

❀ Follow this guide. There are things you'll be instructed to do here that will be followed up on by a leader in a later session. If you get off track, it might affect someone down the line, so be sure you're helping the team by sticking with this guide.

You don't have to have a great singing voice or play a musical instrument to be the Worship Leader at Cozy Mountain Lodge. And we've made it easy for you by selecting songs for each session that clearly relate to and reinforce the lessons everyone will be learning throughout the retreat. The lyrics to these songs are already printed in each woman's Cozy Mountain Lodge Participant Guide, making it easy for everyone!

Hearty Hint

We did our own Cozy Mountain Lodge retreat before putting this book into print because we wanted to make sure everything works. You'll find tips in this book where we share what we learned—and what mistakes we made—so you can have an easier time at your retreat.

You have several options for leading worship. The first option is to play the songs through a sound system and lead the group in singing along with the *Music of Cozy Mountain Lodge* CD. A copy of this CD is included in the Cozy Mountain Lodge Director's Kit, and additional copies are available for purchase. You can still sing into a microphone and let the women hear your voice, but the CD will add fullness to the sound. This is the easiest way to go!

If you prefer live accompaniment, you can use the sheet music provided in this leader guide to sing and play the songs on the instrument of your choice. Or have a whole band and team of singers lead the group in worship.

No matter how you decide to lead, remember that women will take their cues from you. If you're relaxed, enjoying the music, and worshiping, they'll join in wholeheartedly. If you're concerned about "performance," they'll get tense, too. You set the tone.

So make it fun! Encourage each woman to share and celebrate!

Important Legal Information

By purchasing this Cozy Mountain Lodge Worship Leader Guide, you also purchase the right to use the songs and lyrics as often as you like.

But companies that own these songs haven't given you (or us) permission to duplicate these resources. Making your own copies—even to use during a Cozy Mountain Lodge retreat—is against the law, which is a fact many people don't know.

If you plan on having a worship team play the songs for your retreat, you'll need to order extra copies of this book. Extra guides are available from Group Publishing (group.com or 1-800-447-1070) or from your church resource provider.

Women who are attending the retreat will have copies of the lyrics in their Cozy Mountain Lodge Participant Guides, so you don't need to provide those.

Lyrics for all songs

Hearty Hint

Just because you're leading doesn't mean you have to miss out on the fun! When we did Cozy Mountain Lodge ourselves, the Worship Leader found her job was easy enough that she was able to join in with a Getaway Group and participate in all Cozy Mountain Lodge activities. Don't let leading keep you from enjoying this retreat! Join in, and have a great time!

Preparing for Cozy Mountain Lodge!

Get an overview of what's ahead.

Preparation is easy! Here's how to get started:

❀ Attend the training session led by your Cozy Mountain Lodge Director.

❀ Listen to the songs on the *Music of Cozy Mountain Lodge* CD so you know them well.

❀ Read the content for each session several times so you're comfortable making transitions between songs or giving instructions.

❀ Meet with the Session Leaders. You will be involved with several sessions, and it's important for you to work closely with these leaders so there are no miscommunications along the way.

❀ Pray for the women who will attend Cozy Mountain Lodge. Ask God to use you to bring each one closer to him.

It's that simple! Serving as the Cozy Mountain Lodge Worship Leader is as easy as relaxing on the porch swing!

Gather your supplies.

Each time you lead worship, you'll need the following:

❀ Cozy Mountain Lodge Worship Leader Guide*

❀ *Music of Cozy Mountain Lodge* CD*

❀ sound system with microphone and CD player

❀ noisemaker, such as a bell or silly whistle, to use when you need to capture everyone's attention

Hearty Hint

Set up your sound system as early as possible to test for any glitches. And make your job easier by inviting an assistant to run sound for you while you're leading. She can switch songs or adjust sound levels so you can focus on worship.

*One of these is provided in the Cozy Mountain Lodge Director's Kit. Additional copies are available from Group Publishing (group.com or 1-800-447-1070) or your church resource supplier.

The schedule is flexible.

Cozy Mountain Lodge has been created as an overnight getaway. However, it's also flexible for groups that want to use this resource for a shorter one-day gathering or a longer two-night event. The song lists for each session in this leader guide are created for an overnight getaway. If your group is hosting a shorter event, you might want to leave out one song from each session. For a longer, two-night retreat, you may want to add a song to each session. It's up to you.

Partner with the Session Leaders.

One of the great things about Cozy Mountain Lodge is that it doesn't focus on a speaker. Women from your church will lead each of the sessions. Your Director may have one woman lead all sessions, or she may have several different leaders involved. Be sure you touch base with these leaders, whether there's one or seven, before the beginning of the retreat.

You play a key role in helping women focus their hearts on God. But your role is intertwined with that of the Session Leaders. You'll also be sharing sound equipment with these leaders, who are directed to play songs from the CD in the background during times of discussion or to have women listen to a specific song or sound while reflecting on a Bible theme.

When you meet with the Session Leaders, take time to go over an outline of who is leading when and what media needs there are. Look for ways you can partner together and help each other. Take a team approach to make leading easier for each of you!

Warm Welcome – Let music be part of the atmosphere you're creating. Always play music as women are entering and leaving your area. About 10 minutes before each session begins, turn on the *Music of Cozy Mountain Lodge* CD, and let songs play at random while everyone is entering the room. Do the same after each session.

Relax

We know you take choosing songs for a retreat seriously—it's a big responsibility. And just like you, we wondered how women would respond to the songs we chose. Would they like these songs? Would they know them? Would the songs help women go deeper in connecting with the content of the Bible studies? That's why we try everything ourselves before we put anything in print!

It turns out that this mix of praise songs, well-known hymns, and songs written just for Cozy Mountain Lodge was the perfect blend! The newer songs are super-easy to learn, and there were enough familiar elements that everyone was comfortable. And best of all, women really did connect these worship songs with the truths they were learning about in the Bible.

So relax. We've done the hard part for you!

Session 1

This session focuses on choosing God as the firm foundation for our lives. You'll move the women toward this topic as you lead worship, and the Session Leader will deepen the focus on this concept during the session. You'll also be leading everyone in an activity that helps them make new friends and get into their "Getaway Groups," which are the small groups they'll be in for the retreat.

The Cozy Mountain Lodge Director will open this session with a welcome and any announcements. Then she'll introduce you.

Say: **Are you ready for a time of rest and relaxation? A cozy time of warmth and being wrapped in God's love? Well, you're in the right place! Welcome to Cozy Mountain Lodge!**

You received a Cozy Mountain Lodge Participant Guide when you came in today. Hold up a copy of the guide. **This guide has all the song lyrics in it, as well as Bible verses, discussion questions, instructions, and other information we'll use throughout our retreat. You'll want to bring it to every session. We're going to use them right now as we get started with a time of worship.**

One thing most of us love about the mountains is their beauty. Even looking at them from far away reminds us of God's power, majesty, and how beautiful our God is. Let's worship God by singing "Beautiful One." You'll find the words on page 36 of your guide.

Lead "Beautiful One."

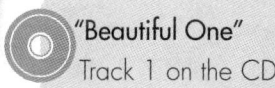
"Beautiful One"
Track 1 on the CD

Say: **During our retreat we're going to be looking at God's faithfulness during the good times in life as well as during those dark and difficult times. Psalm 23:4-5 says, "Even when I walk through the darkest valley, I will not be afraid, for you are close beside me. Your rod and your staff protect and comfort me. You prepare a feast for me in the presence of my enemies. You honor me by anointing my head with oil. My cup overflows with blessings."**

Even when life is hard and we're walking through those dark valleys, God is beside us and pouring blessings into our lives. Those blessings come from God. Let's sing "Blessed Be Your Name," on page 39.

Lead "Blessed Be Your Name."

 "Blessed Be Your Name"
Track 4 on the CD

Say: **One great thing about a retreat is that feeling of getting away from the busyness of life. And it's always more fun to be at a retreat with a few friends. We want to be sure we have time to get to know others while we're here at Cozy Mountain Lodge, so we're going to be in small groups for most of our sessions.**

You'll notice at your table that there are clusters of candles. Four matching candles, to be exact. Pick up the candle closest to you. This is yours to keep—and it's also going to help you get into a small group. In a moment, I'm going to have you find three other women who have candles that are different from yours. You'll get up and move to a new spot, sitting with three other women (so you'll be in a group of four), and none of your candles should match.

When you're sure women understand the instructions, have them pick up their candles and other belongings and move around the room to find a group of four with different candles. Allow a few minutes for everyone to get into their groups. You may need to help a few women find the others with different candles. And remember, *you're* in a Getaway Group, too—so find a group of women now!

It will likely get *very* noisy while the Getaway Groups form. Instead of raising your voice, this is a good time to have a noisemaker such as a bell or silly whistle on hand. Use this instead of yelling. It's a kinder way to get everyone to look back to you when it's time to stop talking!

Hearty Hint

What happens if the numbers don't work out exactly? If you have a few women who simply can't find a group with four different candles, you can just make the decision to let a couple with matching candles be together. If your group doesn't work out to having a number divisible by four, it's OK to have a couple of groups of three people. Please don't allow groups to get larger than four members— we've learned from experience that when groups get bigger, there is less opportunity for sharing.

Say: **Since we're getting away from it all here at Cozy Mountain Lodge, we'll call these groups our Getaway Groups. Take a few minutes to get to know the others in your group by introducing yourself and sharing about a favorite getaway location or vacation spot.**

Allow about 5 minutes for sharing. Play music in the background. When 4 minutes are over, give a 1-minute wrap-up warning.

As we're here at Cozy Mountain Lodge, we're going to be exploring the true source of peace, comfort, and strength. Our key verse is Psalm 46:1, which says, "God is our refuge and strength, always ready to help in times of trouble." This song we're going to sing now reminds us of this passage from the Bible. Let's sing "My Help Comes From the Lord." The lyrics to this song are on page 42.

Lead "My Help Comes From the Lord."

 "My Help Comes From the Lord
Track 7 on the CD

After the song, pray for the leader for this session, for the women who are there, and for God to be honored throughout this retreat. Then introduce the Session 1 Leader. Now it's your turn to have a seat with your Getaway Group and participate with everyone else.

Hearty Hint

During the second session, women do an activity that does not include a time of singing. You get to join in the fun and hang out with your friends!

 *Session 3*

This session focuses on the importance of having supportive Christian friends—and of being that friend, as well. You'll move the women toward this topic as you lead worship, and the Session Leader will deepen the focus on this concept during the session.

With an enthusiastic greeting, welcome women to worship. Say: **Let's start this session by singing praise to God for his awesome creation! You'll find the lyrics on page 43.**

Lead "All Creatures of Our God and King."

 "All Creatures of Our God and King"
Track 8 on the CD

Say: **God is so powerful and strong, so creative and amazing! And what's even more amazing is that he reaches out to us with his love. It makes me want to get to know God more and more. This next song expresses our desire to know God more intimately. It's called "I Want to Know You," and the lyrics are on page 37 of your guide.**

Lead "I Want to Know You (In the Secret)."

 "I Want to Know You (In the Secret)"
Track 2 on the CD

Say: **The more we get to know God, the more we know and experience his love. God loves us so much that he is always with us. Nothing can separate us from God! Psalm 139:7-12 says, "I can never escape from your Spirit! I can never get away from your presence! If I go up to heaven, you are there; if I go down to the grave, you are there. If I ride the wings of the morning, if I dwell by the farthest oceans, even there your hand will guide me, and your strength will support me. I could ask the darkness to hide me and the light around me to become night—but even in darkness I cannot hide from you. To you the night shines as bright as day. Darkness and light are the same to you."**

There is nothing that can keep us from God! Let's sing a song that will be new to many of us, but it's easy to learn. It's called "Nothing Could Keep Me From You," and it's a beautiful reminder of how dear we are to God. The lyrics are on page 41.

Lead "Nothing Could Keep Me From You."

 "Nothing Could Keep Me From You"
Track 6 on the CD

Say: **Let's have open hearts now as we continue to study God's Word.**

Introduce the leader for this session, and then join with your Getaway Group to participate.

Hearty Hint

During Session 4, women will be participating in a service project, so there are no songs to lead during this session. Join in serving others and showing them God's love during Session 4.

Session 5

During this session, women will be discovering more of what it means for Jesus to be our Redeemer and for him to be the shelter of our lives. You'll begin guiding women toward these truths as you lead worship, and the Session Leader will take the concept deeper.

Invite women to join you in worship. Say: **No matter what was happening in their lives, Ruth and Naomi stood firm in their faith in God. Yes, they were discouraged, but they always trusted God. Let's sing "Blessed Be Your Name," praising God for his goodness and faithfulness to us. The lyrics are on page 39 of your guide.**

Lead "Blessed Be Your Name."

 "Blessed Be Your Name"
Track 4 on the CD

Say: **Psalm 33:4 says, "For the word of the Lord holds true, and we can trust everything he does." What a comfort to know that God is reliable and his words are true! Let's sing a new song called "We Can Trust Him," which uses the words of this Psalm. It's easy to learn! You'll find the lyrics on page 40.**

Lead "We Can Trust Him (Psalm 33:4)."

 We Can Trust Him (Psalm 33:4)"
Track 5 on the CD

Say: **Our God is a God of blessing. He is a God of truth and is trustworthy. And he is a God who loves each of us personally. That's worth singing about! Psalm 42:8 reminds us, "Each day the Lord pours his unfailing love upon me, and through each night I sing his songs, praying to God who gives me life." These words remind us of the song "My Help Comes From the Lord." Let's sing that now! The lyrics are on page 42.**

Lead "My Help Comes From the Lord."

 "My Help Comes From the Lord"
Track 7 on the CD

Hearty Hint

During Session 6, women will be participating in a time of prayer and quiet reflection. There is no singing during this session. Enjoy the moments of peace with the rest of the women at your retreat.

After this song, offer a prayer of thanksgiving for the women there and how special they are to you, to each other, and to God! Then introduce the Session Leader and join your Getaway Group.

Session 7

This session wraps up all that has been learned during Cozy Mountain Lodge. *We've switched things around a bit* and put the time of singing at the end of this session. The Session Leader will guide women through a time of Bible reading and discussion, affirmation, and the completion of a keepsake. Then you'll lead a time of worship and celebration. It's a great way to bring this retreat to a close!

Be sure to connect with the Session Leader ahead of time so you can determine how to work together smoothly.

After the Session Leader turns the time over to you, lead women in singing "All Creatures of Our God and King," on page 43 in the guide.

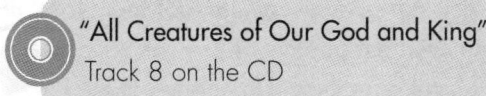

"All Creatures of Our God and King"
Track 8 on the CD

Say: **It's great to praise our amazing Lord! Let's keep that praise going by singing "Beautiful One," on page 36 of your guide.**

Lead "Beautiful One."

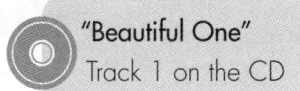

"Beautiful One"
Track 1 on the CD

Say: **It's awesome to think that God, who has created everything, including the majestic mountains, loves us. And it's been great here at Cozy Mountain Lodge to hear words of affirmation from each other, as well. It's precious to be reminded of how special each women here is to God—and to others. In your guide, on page 32, you'll see several verses that remind us of how important it is for us to stand together in support of each other.**

Invite two different women to read these passages aloud
(1 Thessalonians 5:11 and 2 Corinthians 13:11).

Session 7 continued next page!

Say: **Let's sing a song that celebrates our friendships. The words are on page 38.**

Lead "Here for You."

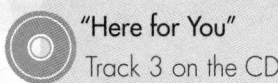

"Here for You"
Track 3 on the CD

Say: **Just as we love and support each other in friendship, God loves and supports us, sheltering us constantly with his grace and mercy. Romans 8:38-39 affirms this, saying, "And I am convinced that nothing can ever separate us from God's love. Neither death nor life, neither angels nor demons, neither our fears for today nor our worries about tomorrow—not even the powers of hell can separate us from God's love. No power in the sky above or in the earth below—indeed, nothing in all creation will ever be able to separate us from the love of God that is revealed in Christ Jesus our Lord."**

Let's sing "Nothing Could Keep Me From You," on page 41 of your guide, as a closing prayer.

Lead "Nothing Could Keep Me From You."

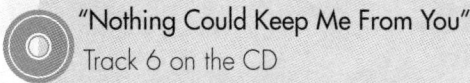

"Nothing Could Keep Me From You"
Track 6 on the CD

Close with a prayer for the women, thanking God for the time together at this retreat and asking for God's hand of blessing on each woman.

If your group wishes to use the evaluations for this retreat, hand them out now and have women complete them before leaving. Your retreat director can print these from the *Graphics & Other Goodies CD*, and the leaders can review them together after the retreat to better understand the needs of women in your church and community.

Thank YOU  for leading worship at Cozy Mountain Lodge!